D0929758

Published by ABDO Publishing Company
8000 West 78th Street, Edina, Minnesota 55439.

Printed in the United States.

Editor: Pam Price
Content Developer: Nancy Tuminelly
Cover and Interior Design:
    Anders Hanson, Mighty Media
Photo Credits: Corbis Images, Garry Gay/Getty Images,
One Mile Up, Marilyn Kazmers/Peter Arnold,
Stockbyte, Shutterstock, Quarter-dollar coin image
from the United States Mint.

Library of Congress Cataloging-in-Publication Data

Lindeen, Mary.
  Griz finds gold : a story about California / Mary Lindeen ;
illustrated by Bob Doucet.
      p. cm. -- (Fact & fable : state stories)
  ISBN 978-1-60453-183-1
  1. California--Juvenile literature. I. Doucet, Bob. II. Title.

F861.3.L56 2009
979.4--dc22
                                    2008017383

Super SandCastle™ books are created by a team of
professional educators, reading specialists, and content
developers around five essential components—phonemic
awareness, phonics, vocabulary, text comprehension,
and fluency—to assist young readers as they develop
reading skills and strategies and increase their general
knowledge. All books are written, reviewed, and leveled
for guided reading, early reading intervention, and
Accelerated Reader® programs for use in shared, guided,
and independent reading and writing activities to
support a balanced approach to literacy instruction.

TABLE OF CONTENTS

Redwood National Park (pg. 4)

California gray whale (pg. 7)

Redding

CALIFORNIA

California dogface butterfly (pg. 11)

Tahoe City

Sacramento

San Jose mission (pg. 12)

Golden Gate Bridge (pg. 8)

Sequoia National Forest (pg. 13)

San Francisco

Fresno

California poppy (pg. 14)

Fruit

California grizzly bear (pg. 4)

Mojave Desert (pg. 17)

Colorado River

San Luis Obispo

orange grove (pg. 17)

tortoise (pg. 17)

Los Angeles

San Diego

LEGEND

☆ CAPITAL   ● STORY START

○ CITY   - - - STORY PATH

⋀⋀ MOUNTAINS   ✖ STORY END

〜 RIVER

California Grizzly Bear

The California grizzly bear is the California state animal. It is the largest, most powerful bear there is. It eats fruits, nuts, fish, and insects. It is on the state flag of California. Hunters killed the last grizzly bear living in California in 1922.

GRIZ FINDS GOLD

It was a warm spring morning when Griz Lee Bear woke up. The tallest trees he had ever seen surrounded him. For a moment, he wondered where he was. Then it all came back to him. He had come from Washington to California to find his fortune. Griz had fallen asleep in Redwood National Park.

His great grandfather had lived in California a long time ago. As a little cub, Griz listened to the grown-ups tell stories about his great grandfather and the gold rush. Griz wanted to find gold like Great Grandpa. Then he'd be rich!

The California Gold Rush

In 1848, a man who worked at a sawmill near Sacramento found gold in the stream. News of the gold soon spread across the country. Starting in 1949, thousands of people rushed to California to find gold of their own. A lucky few became very rich. Most people did not.

Pacific Ocean

The western edge of California is on the Pacific Ocean. This gives California many great beaches. The ocean air makes the weather in some areas of the state perfect for growing crops. Some of these crops are rice, cotton, fruits, and vegetables.

Now that he was awake, Griz smelled the salty air. He headed toward the ocean. The waves sparkled in the sunlight as they washed up on the sand. As Griz walked along the beach, he spotted a large gray whale.

"Well, hello there! I'm Spout," said the whale. "What brings you all the way down here?"

"I'm looking for gold. Do you know where I can find some?" replied Griz.

"Hmmm," Spout said. "I've never seen any gold myself. But I have heard of a golden bridge near San Francisco. You might try there."

"Thanks!" said Griz. As he waved good-bye, Griz saw Spout slap his tail on the water and swim away.

California Gray Whale

The California gray whale is the state marine mammal. Gray whales travel along the coast. They swim to the south in the winter and to the north in the spring. Gray whales weigh 20 to 40 tons. A gray whale has a small hump on its back instead of a fin.

Golden Gate Bridge

San Francisco's famous bridge is one of the longest suspension bridges in the world. It connects San Francisco with Marin County. Sometimes whales swim under the bridge and end up in San Francisco Bay!

Griz headed south. He traveled along the coast. He hiked through mountains and forests. After a long, long walk, he came to a huge bay. There was a big, red bridge across the bay. There was a city on the other side.

Griz made his way across the bridge into the city of San Francisco. It was a very busy place! Griz walked down a very crooked street. He looked at shops in Chinatown. He even rode a cable car! But he didn't see a golden bridge. Finally, he ended up at Pier 39, near Fisherman's Wharf.

San Francisco

The "city by the bay" is famous for foggy weather, Chinatown, and cable cars. It also has Lombard Street. Some people call it the "crookedest" street in the world!

Pier 39

Pier 39 is located on San Francisco's historic waterfront. It has shops, restaurants, and sea lions! The sea lions started spending winters there in 1990. Some winters, as many as 900 sea lions stay there. That's because the bay is full of herring for them to eat.

On Pier 39, he met a sea lion named Sparky. He told Sparky his story and asked her about the golden bridge.

Sparky pointed to the big bridge Griz had come across. "That's the Golden Gate Bridge right there," said Sparky.

"But that isn't gold. It isn't even painted gold," cried Griz.

Griz sat down and started to sob. That's when a butterfly landed right on his nose!

"Please don't cry," said the butterfly. "My name is Breeze. I know where to find flowers made of gold! Follow me." He flew away.

"Wait!" said Griz. "I'm coming."

California Dogface Butterfly

You'll find the beautiful California dogface butterfly only in California. It is also the official state insect of California. The wings of the male butterfly have the shape of a dog's head on them. The female is yellow with a black spot on each wing.

California Missions

In the 1700s, Spanish missionaries traveled from Mexico to California. There, they built 21 missions in 54 years. The towns around the missions grew to become large cities.

After a while, Griz and Breeze stopped for a rest at the old San Jose mission. Griz wondered whether his great grandfather had been there. For a time, the mission was an important trading place for miners.

Griz and Breeze continued on their journey through the California countryside. Breeze led him over hills and past farms.

The giant sequoia is one of the oldest living trees on Earth. They can live for up to 3,200 years. Giant sequoias grow naturally only on the western slope of the Sierra Nevada mountain range. They can grow up to 311 feet tall!

At last, Breeze stopped flying. He sat on a beautiful golden flower. "Well, we made it to Sequoia National Forest," he said. "Here are the flowers made of gold!"

Griz looked at the flowers. They were lovely. They looked like little cups of gold. But they were not gold. They were only flowers.

Breeze was so proud to have helped Griz. Griz didn't want to tell him that the flowers weren't really gold. So he just waved good-bye. Then he lay down and was soon fast asleep.

When Griz woke up, he was very hungry.

California Poppy

Indians used California poppies for food and oil. The flowers grow wild and in gardens all over California. The golden poppy, or cup of gold, is the official state flower. In California, April 6 is California Poppy Day.

Griz sniffed the air. Something off to the west smelled delicious! He followed his nose until he came to a town called Fresno. There he found the sweetest wrinkled fruits and the crunchiest nuts he had ever tasted! He ate until he was full and saved some to eat later on the trail.

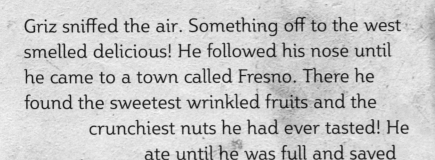

Griz's California Trail Mix

1 cup raisins

1 cup dried apricots

1 cup dried peaches

1 cup walnut halves or almonds

Optional

2 cups granola

1 cup semi-sweet chocolate chips

Mix all the ingredients in a large bowl or a plastic bag. Dig in and enjoy!

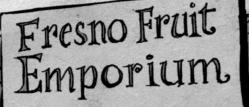

Grapes

Every year, California farmers grow more than 300,000 tons of grapes. Some of the grapes are made into wine. Some of the grapes are sold as fresh fruit. And some of the grapes are dried into raisins. Fresno, in central California, calls itself the raisin capital of the world.

California Quail

The California quail lives in coveys of 10 to 200 birds. You can find it in meadows, forests, and valleys and at the edge of deserts. It is also known as the valley quail. Both the male and the female have a curved, black crown feather on their heads.

As Griz was packing up his trail mix, a bird hopped up to him.

"Hi!" she squawked. "I'm Heather. What brings you to this neck of the woods?"

"Well, I'm looking for gold," Griz replied. "But I'm not having much luck."

"I know of a place where gold is just growing on the trees," chirped Heather.

Griz followed her directions to a huge field of orange trees. He plucked an orange off the tree, peeled it, and took a bite. "These are certainly tasty, but they're not gold either," cried Griz.

Then a large rock nearby started talking to him! "Hey, I'm on my way home to the desert," said the rock. "There's gold there. Would you like to join me?"

The Desert

Southern California has many deserts. One is the Mojave Desert. Another is Death Valley. It is one of the hottest places in the world. The desert is home to many animals, including the desert tortoise. It is the state reptile.

Eureka!

The Greek word *eureka* is the state motto of California. It means "I have found it." Maybe that's what miners said when they found gold! Eureka is also the name of a town in northern California.

Griz discovered that it wasn't a rock at all. It was a tortoise named Shel. Together, they set off for the Mojave Desert. The sunset was flaming orange as they arrived. The sand looked like it was made of gold. "Eureka!" shouted Griz. "I've found it!" The sand slipped through his paws.

"Oh no," he cried. "This isn't gold. It's just sand!"

"I wanted to be rich!" Griz said. "I came all this way for nothing!"

"Are you sure that's true?" asked Shel. "You saw an ocean, mountains, cities, farms, and deserts. You met new friends. You had a great adventure. You didn't find gold, but there are other kinds of riches."

Griz scratched his head and smiled. He realized that his search for gold had indeed made him rich!

THE END

The Golden State

The Golden State became the official nickname for California in 1968. It stands for all the gold that has been found there. It also stands for other golden things in the state, such as the butterflies and the poppies.

CALIFORNIA AT A GLANCE

Abbreviation: CA

Capital:
Sacramento

Largest city: Los Angeles
(2nd-largest U.S. city)

Statehood: September 9,
1850 (31st state)

Area:
163,707 sq. mi.
(423,999 sq km)
(3rd-largest state)

Nickname:
The Golden State

Motto: Eureka

State bird: California quail

State flower:
California poppy

State tree:
California redwood

State marine mammal:
California gray whale

State insect:
California dogface butterfly

State song:
"I Love You, California"

STATE SEAL

STATE FLAG

STATE QUARTER

The California quarter portrays
conservationist John Muir with a
condor flying overhead. The condor,
once almost extinct, symbolizes
California's dedication to conservation.

What Do You Know?

How well do you remember the story? Match the pictures to the questions below! Then check your answers at the bottom of the page!

a. cable car

b. San Jose mission

c. orange trees

d. California gray whale

e. tortoise

f. sea lion

1. What kind of animal is Spout?

2. What did Griz ride on in San Francisco?

3. What animal did Griz meet on Pier 39?

4. Where did Griz and Breeze rest?

5. What did Heather lead Griz to?

6. What kind of creature is Shel?

What to Do in California

1 Explore an Active Volcano

Lassen Volcanic National Park, Mineral

2 Watch a Geyser Erupt

Old Faithful Geyser, Calistoga

3 Ride the Cable Cars

San Francisco

4 See an Aquarium

Monterey Bay Aquarium, Monterey

5 Listen to Jazz Music

Mammoth Lakes Jazz Jubilee, Mammoth Lakes

6 Take the Hollywood Walk of Fame

Los Angeles

7 Visit a Theme Park

Disneyland, Anaheim

8 See Endangered Animals

San Diego Zoo, San Diego

Nevada

Pacific Ocean

Sacramento

CALIFORNIA

Arizona

23

GLOSSARY

cable car – a car pulled along tracks by a strong rope made of many wires or fibers.

herring – a kind of fish that lives in the Atlantic and Pacific oceans.

mammal – a warm-blooded animal that is covered with hair and whose females produce milk to feed the young.

marine – having to do with the sea.

mission – a type of church built to expand the influence and work of a larger church.

missionary – a person who travels to a place to help other people and teach them about his or her religion.

motto – a saying that tells what goals or ideals guide a person or an organization.

pier – a platform that extends over a body of water.

suspension bridge – a bridge with a roadway that is held up by cables attached to tall towers.

About SUPER SANDCASTLE™

Bigger Books for Emerging Readers
Grades K–4

Created for library, classroom, and at-home use, Super SandCastle™ books support and engage young readers as they develop and build literacy skills and will increase their general knowledge about the world around them. Super SandCastle™ books are part of SandCastle™, the leading PreK–3 imprint for emerging and beginning readers. Super SandCastle™ features a larger trim size for more reading fun.

Let Us Know

Super SandCastle™ would like to hear your stories about reading this book. What was your favorite page? Was there something hard that you needed help with? Share the ups and downs of learning to read. We want to hear from you! Send us an e-mail.

sandcastle@abdopublishing.com

Contact us for a complete list of SandCastle™, Super SandCastle™, and other nonfiction and fiction titles from ABDO Publishing Company.

www.abdopublishing.com • 8000 West 78th Street Edina, MN 55439 • 800-800-1312 • 952-831-1632 fax